Althar
Towards Utopia

Joachim Wolffram

The Althar series consists of:
Volume 1: "Althar – The Crystal Dragon"
Volume 2: "Althar – The New Magi"
Volume 3: "Althar – Towards Utopia"
Volume 4: "Althar – The Final Letting Go"

Also available from Joachim Wolffram:
"For You – Records from Your Lives"
"The Free Human"

For information about the author please visit:
www.wolffram.de
or
facebook.com/joachim.wolffram

Contents

1. The No-Place

I am Althar, the Crystal Dragon.

You feel it, don't you? Although I present myself as Althar, I am so much more. I am my true self, I am all the aspects of my true self, and I am an Ambassador of Creation. It is not just a single facet expressing, but it is the essence of all that we are.

And this is so appropriate, because what this text will express is multi-dimensional. It is so beyond the human consciousness, so beyond even human imagination that the sheer attempt of putting it into words seems ridiculous. Nevertheless, what I, with the help of some friends, attempt to bring forth will convey an essence, a scent of the unimaginable. Each individual word will breathe the energy of multi-dimensionality and unfolding.

Yes, I am bragging here on purpose! Why? Because we have to set an appropriate majestic stage! What we are to talk about goes so far beyond petty human thoughts and concepts that "small" or "modest" will not work. Just go with me. Allow yourself to get grand. Allow yourself to shake existence in its very foundations. Because we can. Because *you* can. And because we've been dreaming of it for so long.

After the first series of messages you might have wondered what could come after that. You may have wondered even more after the second series, for in terms of the human imagination, the New Magi seems like the peak of human evolution. *And it is!* That's why I have said those who take that route cease to be humans, although they may still have a human body. But those who can feel will note that a New Magi is no human any more.

In fact, a New Magi might be called a living God. Why? Because he embodies all the attributes humans want a god to have. Deep within, humans remember the totality of the potentials of consciousness, but then assign that to an external entity. The New Magi claims these potentials for himself and embodies them.

But what are Gods doing? Will they continue satisfying minor needs and desires? Will they continue playing energy games? That is where the still limited human is at a loss – occasionally so much so that it even becomes an obstacle. The problem is that *even the imagination of a non-ascended consciousness is limited!*

You might think that the universe you currently imagine is vast. Well, in human terms, it certainly is. But compared to what will become available to a New Magi, this "old" universe is like a grain of sand on an infinitely long beach. Let's take a closer look at this one grain of sand.

Consciousness, true self, was not at peace within and began a frantic search outside of itself. And so it created a rollercoaster ride through a *limited* set of potentials. The non-ascended true selves were searching for themselves, searching for meaning and identity, fighting for energy, fighting for beliefs. They became addicted to ever new distractions. And very quickly, they got caught up in ever the same patterns and cycles. They circled around themselves and were stuck on that single, tiny grain of sand, without having any idea of the beach's existence. This is why it is said creation approached a standstill! And if you were creation, wouldn't you say at some point, *"Enough! Enough with all of those repetitions!"*

The fear of a standstill was felt by many beings. But it was a misconception! It was not some outer force, entity, or mechanism that would have driven creation to a standstill. *It would have been the entities themselves,* because they could not find a way out of their externalizations. In a sense, you might say the entities would have gone into a meltdown, completely exhausted after eons of repetitive experiences. They would have entered a state of autism – not venturing out any more, but not being at peace within either.

With the advent of embodied ascension, that has changed fundamentally! Through this it became clear that the expansion of consciousness would continue on an on. The gods, who have sprung from human imagination, may play human games. The *real* Gods though, *the ascended true selves,* soar way beyond human imagination. They explore the whole beach.

These messages are meant for those who are setting out to take a walk on the beach. They are for those who are on the brink of becoming a New Magi. The way to realization is arduous at times, so some uplifting support may be helpful. This is why we feel now is the time to lift the veil and convey as best we can what awaits the New Magi.

This undertaking is quite ambitious, because the still limited human consciousness just cannot imagine an existence that is no longer based on the desire for externalization or reflection. However, a New Magi in the becoming is going more and more beyond any limitation, and hence, becomes receptive at his very core to a new way of existing.

Thus, in this third series we will speak of *Utopia*. We will speak of what awaits you once you set yourself free, once you venture beyond the search for self and limited desires into true freedom and unlimited creatorhood.

Utopia literally means "no-place". What an appropriate term to denote the worlds beyond limitation. Utopia is most certainly not some humanly heaven or some community where everyone behaves nicely.

Utopia is not a fairy tale. It is neither science fiction nor fantasy. Rather, Utopia already exists and the gateway to Utopia is wide open to you. *This is why* you embodied on Earth. *This is why* you are attracted to enlightenment and ascension.

For a very long time Utopia has been just a dream, but meanwhile the realization has set in that *Utopia* surpasses even the wildest of dreams.

*

Dear reader, at a certain point you have to make a choice so deep within your true self that it will affect all realities experienced by all the emanations of your true self. That choice will set free an omniverse of new potential intents. Never again will you limit your experiences to that tiny grain of sand. Instead, you will join the Third Round of Creation and explore Utopia.

The first series was a preparation and had a strong flavor of clarity and compassion. It invited you to get rid of your body of un-consciousness, your emotional body. Furthermore, I introduced some concepts that were needed along the way. The second series was more technical and provided insights into *how* consciousness creates. It outlined the way for the New Magi and embodied ascension. This third series reaches beyond consciousness as the human knows it. Therefore, it should be no surprise that the chapters to come will not provide any instructions or detailed maps to reach Utopia. Instead, just rely on the natural ability of consciousness to come into harmony with what has already been experienced. We will say more about this later.

This text is certainly not for everyone. If you feel any resistance right now, consider coming back to it later. But if you are ready to soar into the beyond, then come! Come and join me right now! How? Just *feel*, then *fall* into the knowingness that is all around you right now.

Let us now begin by bringing in Aouwa, my true self, who has patiently waited until this moment. Let Aouwa speak directly to your own true self by shifting your perspective from the human reading this text to your true self, which is before every appearance.

I am Althar, an Ambassador of Utopia.

2. The Point Before Creation

I am Aouwa, a true self in expression.

When I came into existence, I was empty. Empty of anything. Empty of identity. Empty of knowingness. Empty of relations. Empty of dependencies. Even empty of wisdom.

Suddenly I *was*. Suddenly I was aware of myself as existing. Where did I come from? I had no clue. Why did I come into existence? I could not say, nor think, nor feel.

Of course, at that point I had no notion of "I". Within me, there were no notions or abstractions whatsoever. It was the empty me finding myself in the midst of emptiness. The human cannot relate to this in any way. The human thinks of being lost. But how can you get lost if you have no body? The human thinks of darkness. But how can it be dark without having the experience of light? The human thinks of abandonment. But what would that mean if you do not know anything other than the awareness of yourself?

Dear reader, dear true self, you too had this original experience. Indeed, every true self went through it and has subsequently passed on this original uncertainty to *all* its creations and emanations.

I invite you now to return as best as possible to this original feeling of pure awareness of your beingness. Even if you say you have no recollection of it, try it anyway. How? Just become aware of your existence *without any characteristics!* Do not cling to any form and feel the ultimate relaxation coming with it. Do not hold on to any belief, for beliefs form realities. Also, there is no need to fear extinguishing yourself, because this is simply impossible. You tried that before, remember?

In fact, being aware of this deepest depth of yourself *is the only natural thing in all of existence.* Everything else is created. But the *you without characteristics,* to which I am speaking right now, was *not* created.

Did you get back there? Good.

I call this the point before creation.

Can you fathom this? *Before* creation, *yet you are.* "How can that be?" you ask.

It is, because *you are creation.* It is, because creation is not something "out there". Creation is nothing else but *you in expression.*

*

In that respect, all true selves are equal. Still, every true self is its own creation, because it has its unique point before creation *which belongs to it and to it only.* Therefore, your existence, just as that of any other true self, is *unique,* although it is not special in any way. It is not larger, nor grander, nor more potent than the existence of any other true self. I do not say this out of a desire for egalitarianism, but from experience.

I use the term "point before creation" as a synonym for true self, for it particularly emphasizes that the true self exists beyond all creation.

The moment you became aware of your existence is seemingly of unparalleled importance for you. Nonetheless, there is another moment having at least the same significance. Perhaps it has already happened for you and you are reading this text just to have some companionship or to get an alternate perspective. Or perhaps this second moment still lies in the future of your stream of experiences. If the latter is the case for you, rest assured that you cannot miss this moment. *It will find you!* I shall speak about this particular moment soon, but before I can do that, we need a similar understanding of the history of creation.

For this, come again to your point before creation. Open completely into the awareness of your true self. Something has changed since you originally awakened to your existence. Can you feel it? It is like something has been added to the original consciousness of yourself.

I call this something *wisdom*. Even though you may *remember* how your true self felt in the very beginning of your existence, you cannot really return there, because in the meantime you have gathered wisdom. This wisdom is not like a sack of golden nuggets or pearls stored in some hidden chamber of your true self. Not at all! Instead, every piece of wisdom you gained, even every experience you made, has changed not only your true self, but has also *changed creation itself.*

A true self cannot un-experience what it once experienced. It cannot un-know. It cannot un-wisdom its wisdom. A true self may reach new interpretations and perspectives of what it has experienced, but experienced will remain experienced forever. In this sense, creation can never go backwards.

I like to view wisdom as a kind of resume that a true self draws from its very personal perspective. Once a certain piece of wisdom is present, the *true self feels less or no desire to repeat the related experiences.*

Now, from the perspective of your true self, have a look at your human life and how it unfolded up to this now moment. Take a little time and condense the experiences of your life more and more, until you have a single comprehensive feeling representing this lifetime. If you like, create a resume.

*

This multi-dimensional, multi-faceted feeling represents the essence of all your experiences of this lifetime. *It is the wisdom of your life.*

If you look at the life of one of your emana-tions from your point before creation, then a natural acceptance for all facets of this emanation arises. The true self knows about the non-reality of every reality. It does not identify with a life story, but is enriched by its experiences, no matter what kind of experiences these are. Through this acceptance of the true self, experiences are transformed into wisdom. Only the limited human has difficulties accepting himself in his totality, and therefore often becomes a prisoner of his experiences.

Now that you are within your true self, marvel at the wisdom you have gathered. It is the result of all the experiences you have made, in whatever form or reality, since you first became aware of your awareness. Again, if you like, create a resume. A resume of the entire Second Round of Creation, as you have experienced it.

*

One could say that the original sparks of creativity lit up very early in creation when we, the true selves, made our very first baby steps into external existence. Back then, we all ran out to have experiences and to come to know what this "creation" was all about. We had the passion of newborn babies wanting to discover their environment. We brought some potentials to life without knowing *how* we did that. Then we used our imagination to rearrange and experience these potentials in all their diversity and variability.

And that is exactly what we repeated again and again. Variation after variation after variation of the same potentials. Eon after eon after eon.

At some point though, we became aware that imagination does not exactly create anything new.

Although imagination is a wonderful tool, it is based on what has already been. In essence, it just repeats, refines, prolongs, and rearranges the already experienced. Imagination creates *quantity*. It provides details and definitions. But imagination cannot birth any new *quality*.

Imagination is limited, and so our experiences remained limited.

Before you continue on to the next chapter, I invite you to feel into the deeper implications of this finding. What does it mean to exist for eons and then to suddenly realize that even though you are a creator, everything you do is just a repetition, refinement, extension, and rearrangement of ever the same potentials?

I am Aouwa.

3. The Standstill

I am Aouwa, a true self in expression.

As explained by Althar in the previous volume, at a certain point the true selves discovered their ability to have intents. Moreover, in an alchemistical transmutation they brought forth pure energy to reflect these intents so that the true selves could perceive them. After that, it didn't take long for the true selves to discover each other and start co-creating.

Furthermore, they began playing energy games amongst themselves; arm wrestling and power struggles, just like kids on the playground. And why wouldn't they? The entities, you, me – we didn't know any better. After all, there was neither pain nor death, as a human knows it. It was all about coming to know what could be done as consciousness having intents and pure energy at its disposal.

In the course of time, the entities grouped together. The groups were partly based on common preferences and interests, and partly on pure coincidences, just like human children still experience it today. Your best friend usually lived around the corner, just as the peers of your clique did. Had you been growing up in a different spot, you would have been with another group, not even noticing the implications. Even what eventually became the spiritual families can be traced back to this era.

The formation of groups is one of the main characteristics of the Second Round of Creation. Isn't that interesting? How can it be that equally potent and indestructible true selves sought refuge in a community?

Well, because each of them feared their own point before creation. They feared that initial trauma of discovering their existence, not knowing anything about themselves. They feared getting "mad" in their own void. Therefore, anything was better than staying "inside". But on the "outside" there were others, there were distractions, so groups came into existence and with them came group dynamics.

The moment a few entities agree on any topic, their perspective of reality is solidified. Then they stick to their beliefs all the more, assuming they cannot be that wrong as long as their beliefs are shared by others. *And it feels so good!* So much better than being alone in the void. Many latecomers who accidentally encountered a group simply took on the group's beliefs just to become a member of a community.

Of course, a group is not just a place of shelter; it is also the perfect place to explore the mechanics of energy and energy feeding. One does this either by finding some position and identity inside one's own group, or by confronting other groups for their ridiculous beliefs.

Both the individual fear, as well as group affiliations and their resulting dynamics are present *to this very day* for the vast majority of entities.

You might say this all sounds so human, so predictable, so incredibly shallow. And that is exactly what it is! Quite frankly, humans experience it even in a weakened form. Imagine how these dynamics unfold in non-physical realms that are not based on time. In realms where instantaneous manifestation happens. In a setting where each intent is automatically played out. Can you imagine a power struggle in such an environment? A dispute? A conflict between groups? A war? Imagine for a moment, all the human thoughts you have while engaged in a conflict instantly manifesting!

So energy feeding and destruction were and are just as much a foundation for groups as caring and sharing. As we will see later, it seems that it had to be that way. The true selves were just exploring and acting out potentials which were based on *polarity*.

However, as mentioned in the previous chapter, at some point the entities noticed that all they were doing was basically just a repetition, refinement, prolongation, and rearrangement of already created building blocks, be they energetic or conceptual. This insight became more and more sinister to the true selves in general and in particular to many group leaders and influencers.

For how often can you play the same game? Remember, there is no death in those realms. Can you imagine doing the tasks you are doing in your human life right now for the rest of eternity? Even if you felt like being in a pleasant environment, how much wine can you drink? How much sex can you have? How much music can you compose? How many people can you rule? How many details can you discover? How often can you move in a circle until you say, "Enough!"?

All these things are seductive only from a relative standpoint, accompanied by the ticking of a running clock. It could be worse, right? So it seems best to enjoy what you have. But I do not speak in terms of some remaining years until your human body wears out. I speak of *eternity*, of *eternal* repetition. Yes, even beyond time there is eternity.

"What do you want to experience today?"

"Why not have some wine? That would be awesome."
"Cool. Sounds exciting."
Really?

When it became apparent that this way of creation did not provide any new creativity, there was the very justified fear that the entities would become crazy. They had lost themselves in their externalizations without finding any true or lasting fulfillment. Lacking any idea for a "way out", lacking the understanding of what was really going on, some started to withdraw. They stopped "going out" and instead retreated more and more. They ceased to partake in any co-creation. However, this was not done in a healthy or curious way to explore their true selves, but in order to escape the outer realities.

Try to feel into a true self just before it enters such a state. It is trapped in ever the same cycles. Trapped in patterns, repeating itself over and over again at a rapid pace without producing anything new. At some point, total withdrawal seems to be the only acceptable choice. Consciousness collapses and encloses itself within itself.

Those who had taken that route brought all their experiences with them; not just the pleasant ones, but also their fears, frustrations, expectations, and sorrows. They closed themselves up inside their personal realm like in a private museum, without ever letting anything fresh in. They used their creative powers only to remain there and no longer have to feel the "exterior". This was not a free choice, but a melt-down out of pure exhaustion.

Such a true self is in the state of a crippled God. A God nonetheless, *but caught within itself.* A God in depression, not using its innate creative abilities.

In other words, *a God at a standstill.*

*

If things went dark and the energy dropped into a bottomless pit, then I was happily successful in making my point clear. To lighten up the mood again, I remind you that ultimately, these are just experiences which do not require any judgment. *Even a God caught within himself is part of the spectrum of potential experiences!* So some entities gave it a try, even if they may have done so unconsciously.

21

Sooner or later, all of these beings will get out of their condition. Why? *Because that is the nature of polarity!* Because at some point they will get curious again and begin to sneak out of their personal realm. They will then discover that in the meantime, something great has happened in creation.

Do you remember the story of Althar, the Atlantean? He had gotten into a similar state by using his creative abilities to enclose himself in a small bubble of his own consciousness. He did this out of the shock that came over him in the face of events he believed he had triggered. He let himself be carried away by despair and his feelings of guilt and shame. But ultimately, he was "only" a sphere within the infinite sphere of my own.

On the level of me, his true self, his choice and experiences contributed to gaining insight into the underlying dynamics. Ultimately, you might say it was *necessary* to recognize what can happen even to an awakened consciousness when it reconnects too closely with the human realm. So he has helped to inspire many others *not* to follow his example in post-enlightenment. You see, events always have many facets, even if they appear to be tragic from the human point of view.

I repeat, once an entity experiences something, others can relate to that. They do not need to experience it themselves. Creation in its entirety changes with every experience.

And so there was this very real impasse in creation. Everything went into repetition and was approaching exhaustion. Some were more conscious of this than others; some deny it to this very day. But overall a consensus was established amongst the entities that there was a huge probability for "The Standstill" to happen. So the question arose, what could be done to avert it.

Althar, the Crystal Dragon, has already spoken about those who had discovered the "Principle of Ascension". They had realized ascension beyond the physical; they came to fully accept their respective true self as their point before creation, as the principle of creation itself. They ceased to need any external reflections of themselves in order to create some false identities. They came to be at peace *within* themselves. *Unconditional peace!* Beyond a need for identity.

Alas, they have hardly been able to raise this potential in other true selves, mainly for three reasons: First, it was too simple. The others could not accept that something so important was so easy to realize. Second, it involved facing the initial trauma of becoming aware of oneself while being in emptiness. Third, there was a tiny, tiny spark of doubt left within them which could be felt by the others.

Nevertheless, when it came to searching for ways to bypass the standstill, they suddenly got more attention. As lofty and ungraspable as the idea of ascension sounded, it still gave some hope for both a new way of existence and for the birth of entirely new potentials. Some even spoke of the "Third Round of Creation". Sovereign beings in their full creatorhood, who had overcome their deeply anchored un-knowingness, caused by fear and denial of their own true self, and could thus bring forth undistorted creativity.

Let's pause with that. I feel like an old grandpa telling a story to his great-grandchildren. So just recall, dear reader, you are no younger than I am. You were a part of that story just as I was. And the happy ending will be experienced by us together. It has already begun, so to speak.

I am Aouwa.

4. Towards Utopia

I am Aouwa, a true self in expression.

Much has been said about the dream of embodied ascension, and it has been assigned to various time periods throughout human history. But the fact is, this dream was born shortly after physical matter was created.

As explained by Althar in a previous message, creation in the non-physical realms is very fleeting and kind of fuzzy. There is no real pause between an intent and its manifestation, or between a cause and its effect, as humans would say. Therefore, insights gained in the non-physical realms tend to be fleeting and fuzzy also. Because of this, they are often times doubted by the very beings that had those insights. Are they "real"? Are the conclusions "correct"? Observing while being the creator is not a simple thing. It is like wanting to swim without creating waves in the water.

That is why the creations of time, space, and physical reality were such breakthroughs. Isn't that peculiar? Physical matter represents the very end of the spectrum of energy. It is highly compressed and structured. Yet, as your scientists know, *it is still fuzzy!* You cannot grab the building blocks of energy, because *there are none!* At least not in a way that humans could make any sense of it. As the mind progresses deeper, it continues to create more details, but it will never reach a point where the question, "How?" could not be asked.

Yet, physical matter, in conjunction with time and space, became the prime laboratory for researching creation itself. In a physical realm, an intent needs time to unfold. It requires time for the energies to arrange themselves accordingly. Moreover, in a co-created realm, other entities might have conflicting intents and undermine some manifestations. Or, on the contrary, multiple entities may be required to manifest a certain intent. In any case, everything happens at a much slower speed, leaving room for the creator to fully experience how intents and energies work together. Furthermore, the reduced speed allows for true contemplation of one's own actions and reactions.

The creation of physical reality was a milestone in the history of consciousness as we know it. There was no way for us to predict its existence or what would develop from it. It was a creative act in conjunction with passionate explorations, and well, a good dose of fortune. To be honest, it started accidentally when two entities had some non-physical scuffle. They smashed energies into each other and suddenly, oops, there was some *particle*. Unheard of! Never seen before! Others rushed in and soon many entities joined forces to explore the latest thing in creation.

The physical reality thus began with a single particle, which created by chance. Others might tell the story differently, but I like this version, simply for the humor that lies in it. And it makes it very clear that it was certainly not planned by an all-knowing and almighty God. It was just kids playing on some playground, gauging their potency.

After the initial discovery of a particle, soon various versions of physical reality were created and explored on a large scale. Although this gave rise to new and more stable insights about consciousness, it did not take long until this very new creation of physical reality was used to act out the same old story lines, only using denser energies. And so, what was absolutely new, very quickly became something old.

When the question of how to avoid the looming standstill became more and more pressing, the idea of embodying in physicality was born. If some entities *embedded* themselves into a physical body, maybe that perspective would allow for new creativity and new potentials of consciousness. Because this would allow these entities for the very first time to really be *within* their own creations and to experience them in *slowness*. And the vision went even further: If in addition, the embodied portion of a true self could be made *to forget its origin,* then it would be even more revolutionary and promising. For this would be a replication of the true self having to cope with a completely alien environment. Who could know what these embodied, isolated beings would discover?

Now imagine the excitement of those who had already realized non-embodied ascension.

Wouldn't physical reality be *the* place to verify *and validate* their insights in super-slow motion? Maybe it was even a means to inspire other entities to also come to realize their own true selves!

So the dream of embodiment sounded new, exciting, and promising to many – albeit for different reasons. And in its wake came the *dream of embodied ascension.*

It took millions and millions of years to prepare Earth, to create biology, plants and animals, and to develop patterns that allowed life forms to survive and replicate themselves. For a human such a time span seems quite long. How can one spend such a long time simply preparing something if "The Standstill" is looming in the background? But here we are talking eons and probabilities, not human time frames. Also, we are beyond time, which in this case, worked for us.

At some point the circumstances were right and slowly, slowly, the first true selves sent morsels of their consciousness into the various beings on Earth.

A human consciousness cannot fathom the magnitude of this undertaking. How could the non-physical and physical come together and coexist? It is like attempting to combine fire and water. That was a *grand* challenge.

Even though I spoke of the true selves as being like kids on the brink of puberty, this was not meant to be degrading in any way. Recall your own childhood. That was when you had unlimited passion, when you did not worry about tomorrow, and when you took risks without even noticing them. So it was the impetuous passion of the creator beings that made many of us tackle the challenge of bringing together consciousness and matter. Eventually, we concentrated our efforts mainly on the human species and experimented until all the necessary details had been created.

And then, suddenly, it happened. The dream of embodiment became real.

So we made it. *You* made it. And here we are. With embodiment came an unparalleled new and deeper understanding of consciousness, and most importantly for me, and I suppose for you:

Even the dream of embodied ascension became real!

*

If you change the perspective of the limited human to the timeless true self, and then review the history of creation as we have just done, it is obvious that individual details are not really important. Not even the individual stories of all your or my incarnations, or the occurrences in your current human life up to this point are of real significance.

Seen from this all-encompassing viewpoint, only one thing really matters: that you are aware of your true self and at the same time have a human body!

*

After this long preparation we can now try an experiment. During the experiment, stay aware of your true self and your human body at the same time.

Imagine your true self as being a sun. A *huge* sun. Then stay with that feeling.

*

Now enter with your human consciousness into that sun. Move deep into the sun's fire. Even if the sun is tremendously large, go right to its center. Here it is hot. A few million degrees. Nothing human can withstand this temperature. Allow everything you brought with you to dissolve into the heat and become part of the sun itself. Take some time to let the fire free you from whatever you are holding onto. Relax into it. Relax into yourself.

*

Do you notice? You are losing all form, but still *you are!* Now that you have let go of all form, you are one with the sun, one with this grand sphere of energy. Take some time to feel your immensity and how you emit rays in all directions.

*

Now sense your human body – how it sits on Earth reading this text. Let a ray of your sun touch this human.

*

I ask you this: *Who are you?* Are you the sun? Or the ray? Or the human? What feels the most real for you?

*

Now imagine how you as a sun retract all of your rays. You stop radiating. You stop going *out there.* You contract further and further until you are just a point. Then *fall* through this point!

*

Aah! *You still exist!* You, your true self, does not need to create in order to exist. You exist *before* any creation, *before* any externalization. And you are rich in wisdom. Wisdom you have distilled from all of your experiences and from the experiences of all of creation.

Here you are *complete!* Nothing is lacking, no part of you is missing. Can you feel it?

Here you are *safe!* Nothing can harm you. Can you feel it?

If you can feel it, if it is an experienced know-ingness, then you have set yourself free!

This is your true self in freedom. *This is you.*

All questions have vanished. Even "Who am I?" has dissolved.

*

Now, with that acceptance of your true self, with that deep, deep feeling of having come home, shine once again. Let your rays go out. Once again, let a ray touch your human body who is just reading this text.

Do you notice?

Do you?

*

A human, whose consciousness is making his way back to his true self in full acceptance of himself, beyond any doubt, beyond any fear, and beyond any lack, transmutes his true self *in its entirety*. All the rays of his true self are changed instantly. All of his emanations in whatever form or shape, in whatever reality or time are immediately touched.

Such a true self has reached the point where non-distorted creation becomes available to him. Creation without any agenda, without any need for mirroring himself. Totally new potentials are accessible to him, and so one can say:

The standstill is overcome by embodied ascension.

*

Just as physical reality began with a single particle, so did embodied ascension start with a single being, followed by some more beings, and some more, and some more.

The dream of embodied ascension has been realized. Maybe some of you will experience it together while being incarnated in the same time-space reality. But no matter how you choose to experience it and how long you choose to stay embodied, know that embodied ascension will become a reality for you. Why? Well, guess why you are attracted to this outlandish text? *You are one of those dreamers who have kept this dream alive for eons.*

*

Maybe, just maybe, the time has come for you to wake up from the dream and to live it. Maybe it is time to take a step back, to look at the Second Round of Creation *in its entirety* and to transmute it into your very personal wisdom.

The moment you do that – the moment you choose to end the dream so it can become a living reality for you – will be of equal magnitude as your original coming to awareness of yourself. One might say, this will be *your original birth.*

You birth yourself and grant yourself full sovereignty.

Whatever happened before was just a preparation, a dance in the womb of limitation; sometimes a frantic search, sometimes a joyous celebration, but mostly it was repetition, refinement, rearrangement, and prolongation of what had already been. But now, after all these experiences, you approach your first real birth. You are standing on the doorway to the Third Round of Creation. What an adventure.

Perhaps the standstill was just a big illusion. Perhaps it was only a way for consciousness to challenge itself into making the next quantum leap in its own unfolding. But the fact is, that leap has occurred. The Third Round of Creation has already begun. Here we call it *Utopia*, as that term is more handy, less technical, and has some beautiful human connotations.

Dear friend, even though you have to make the last non-steps on your own, what could be more beautiful than walking a part of the way with you?

It was a great honor and joy for me to be with you and to talk about everything that was. Now let's head towards Utopia.

I am Aouwa.

5. Beyond Nirvana

I am Althar.

Today I am coming in as a collective. A collective consisting not only of some facets of my true self, but also of other entities.

A collective of humans is usually understood as a group trying to achieve something together, whereby each individual is required to step back and let go of personal interests. In contrast, a collective of ascended beings is an ad hoc composite of consciousness. A composite of true selves, who are beyond any need to act out their personalities. In such a composite, there are simply no classical group dynamics involved. The beings come together for various reasons and for limited periods of no-time to create together, to experience together, or – as in right now – to convey a certain energy together.

Moreover, a collective of ascended beings, of *sovereign* beings, is totally different from a swarm-like collective of beings who have surrendered to a group and have either denied or not yet experienced their individuality.

Utopia is a difficult topic to talk about, so here we come as a collective to convey a feeling of Utopia beyond all words. Imagine us as an orchestra, accompanying one or two flutes playing in the foreground.

Turning towards Utopia feels like trying to look into the sun. The brightness hurts the eyes and the head wants to turn away. And actually, this image is very accurate. The potential of Utopia is so bright, so beyond the limited human consciousness, that the eyes and the mind fear becoming overpowered by it.

Only those who have realized their true self will be able to fully open up to the brightness radiating from Utopia. That is why we have visited a sun in the previous chapter and also in the first book. This was no coincidence, but a preparation.

Over the last years you might have accustomed yourself more and more to that brightness, but in any case, trust your reflexes and shut your inner eyes at the right time, because, well, you *could* be overpowered. Not necessarily while reading this text, but while you are on your own and opening up more and more.

Amongst those who are with us today is the one who I love to call the archetype of enlightenment: Shakyamuni Buddha. Shakyamuni was a wise one. So wise that he refused to talk about anything that came after enlightenment. His conviction was that this kind of information would simply not be helpful for his followers. They would just get distracted and flee into new illusions, making it even more difficult for them to realize enlightenment.

Was he right? He thinks so, considering the times back then. Your contemporary time is quite different in many ways though. One might say that it is more difficult than ever to realize enlightenment. Why? *Because of the widespread loss of the ability to be in stillness.* Without stillness, without the ability to turn within and let go of any outer distractions, *realization will just not happen.* However, the ones to whom this text will find its way do not lack stillness, and therefore, they should be able to deal wisely with the information.

So even if speaking about Utopia could become a new distraction for some, we still feel it will be a support for many others. An aid to stay on their chosen path of realizing embodied ascension.

Our wish is to make it very clear that *enlightenment is not a dead end,* as many tend to think of it. It is not a boring existence in an otherwise crazy cosmos. *Instead, enlightenment is the doorway to Utopia.*

Shakyamuni was groundbreaking for human consciousness in so many ways. He left his family and gave up his very prestigious social status. He permeated and rejected the doctrines of his time and then continued his search on his own in a rather extreme manner. When he was completely exhausted and only a breath away from physical death, he finally gave up his search. He let go of his ascetic exercises and his ideas of awakening. And only a few days later, after he had regained some physical strength, he suddenly realized enlightenment.

And then? What should he do? Remain incarnated and expose himself to the hardship of his time? He did not believe that he could convey his realization. But when he got the insight that there might be a few who could be ready, he decided to stay. He was able to remain incarnated for some forty years, in which, without ceasing, he taught those who strived for true liberation.

Shakyamuni did not compromise. His whole life and teachings were devoted exclusively to enlightenment. It was his complete openness which enabled him to become acquainted with the unlimited, and thereby to gain deep insights into the nature of reality and consciousness. And it was his utmost compassion that enabled him to stay incarnated and to be in service to those who were interested in his teachings, despite all the difficulties he had to face.

As profound and liberating as his teachings have been, it was first and foremost his personal presence, his aura, his embodiment of stillness that turned the most talented seekers of the time into his disciples. When they saw him, they just *knew* Shakyamuni went beyond conditional existence. They just *knew* Shakyamuni was right when he proclaimed, he had set himself free. And so some of the most prominent spiritual leaders of his time gave up their own schools and joined him. Yes, it was a grand time, a grand movement. It was a breakthrough in human consciousness that is impactful to this very day.

One afternoon, Shakyamuni was sitting with his disciples in a forest. A monk asked him, "Shakyamuni, did you tell us all that you have realized? Or are you holding something back?"

Shakyamuni took a handful of leaves and said: "See the leaves in my hand. This much I have told you. Now see the leaves in all the trees around us. This much I have realized."

"But why do you not reveal everything to us?" asked the monk.

"Because what I am talking about helps you to realize your own liberation, and then you can see for yourself. What I'm not talking about would just be a distraction."

Shakyamuni has always refused to define Nirvana, because any definition would immediately be a limitation. The furthest he went was stating that Nirvana is the end of all kind of annoyances. Since he was not even willing to say more about Nirvana, he certainly did not talk about something like "Beyond Nirvana".

His refusal to answer metaphysical questions has made his teachings very difficult for the average person. But he simply did not want to feed the curious, limited mind, knowing that nothing he could say would ever satisfy the mind's thirst for more. Only experiencing what Shakyamuni had experienced himself would accomplish this miracle. Thus, he refused to talk not only about Nirvana, but also about everything metaphysical.

With this introduction, we wanted to prepare the stage as a collective and once again make it clear that we are walking on very thin ice. Utopia is not for the human to imagine. Our words are not meant to satisfy the curious human mind or to become the next spiritual carrot dangling just before the mouths of the humans. We convey a bit of Utopia's essence in service to those who are on their way to embodied ascension.

Now, please welcome Shakyamuni.

*

I greet you, dear human, who is approaching the highest form of consciousness. What do I mean by "highest"? I mean a consciousness that is free of limitations, that has even let go of the notion of *self*, yet continues to be aware of its individuality.

I remember very well my lives as a human being, so I assume a human form while you are with me.

See my hand. See the leaves I am holding. I ask you: Are you ready to see for yourself? Are you willing to let go of each and everything you currently hold on to? Are you? Good. I trust you. So please, come with me. We will have a walk.

Have you ever walked next to a Buddha? You certainly know, Buddha just means "awakened". It is not so special. You can become a Buddha every moment, and indeed, as a human, that is the only way – going from a moment of being awake to the next moment of being awake. Everyone is capable of doing it. So please, be in no way intimidated when walking next to me. I am just a version of your future.

In my last lifetime I taught my monks to either speak of the true reality and how to realize it, or not to speak at all. Well, rules need to be flexible, so today I will speak as I wish.

First, let me share what a burden it was for me *not* to speak about all the leaves in the trees. Back then, I had seen breathtaking universes. I felt into what you call the future. I went out and taught the Gods. Can you imagine? You might feel humbled walking next to me, but I went out to the grandest and most powerful deities and told them they were imprisoned in their imaginations, whereas I had managed to liberate myself. And guess what: *Some even listened!* Thereupon, some were so courageous to incarnate on Earth. Well, maybe you are one of those Gods I talked into incarnating, hmmh? You never know. Or do you?

If there is something that most humans have in common, it is the tendency to feel less than being a God. But how does one become a God? By believing it. But beliefs of any kind are not meant to be taken seriously. They are just a means to experience oneself.

Back then, I was lucky though. I had the honor to share my time with some of the most profound humans who ever lived on Earth. They were nearly enlightened even before they met me. Maybe they were just lacking a bit of rebellious no-self-consciousness. Maybe they just needed to be around someone who proclaimed himself to be enlightened. Whatever the reason, some realized enlightenment and became equals to me. So actually we were a team of realized beings, and thus it became easier for all of us to stay embodied and to stay amongst humans.

While I distract you with my stories from the past, open up. Feel where we are walking. See for yourself. Breathe in the essence of the realm we are just crossing.

Humans just cannot imagine a life worth living without challenges. They prefer longing for love through others rather than loving themselves. They prefer fearing the future rather than letting go of the idea of death. When looking at the rich and super-rich, they see evidence every day that material abundance does not produce any lasting satisfaction. Yet, they crave money and apparent security. And then they ask the enlightened beings if their lives are not completely boring.

Well, no, they are not. Why? Because we have no life in the sense that you think of lives. We come and go as we like, meaning we go in and out of expression as we wish. Actually, that was the preferred title I used back then for myself when I walked the Earth. The *Tathagata*. Thus come, thus gone. Coming from suchness. Going into suchness. Isn't that beautiful? Back then, I did not use the terms "I" or "me". Instead, I referred to myself as the Tathagata. You see, although I had a physical body, I wanted to make it clear that I was not a human any longer. And I played my role very well.

Today, I was invited to come. Thus, I came. We are having a walk. We will say our goodbyes.

Thus, I go. Into the formless without leaving a trace, other than maybe a fine scent that you might take with you.

So, just let go of the notion of life. There is no life after entering Nirvana. *Life and freedom cannot coexist.*

Oops. That's a big one to swallow, right?

Yes, hard to accept for a human clinging on to his life, but an utter no-brainer for a non-human, having transcended life and thus, thankfully, his brain.

The good news is that you can *have* a life and be free. But if you believe you *are* your life, well, then you might want to dig into my teachings. They are certainly not outdated and might cure you from any limitations.

Keep walking with me. Stop thinking. Have you noticed? It is peaceful out here. If I had to choose one attribute of Utopia to which a human can relate, then I would choose *peace*.

You will not encounter any entity in Utopia that *wants* something from you, or that is not at peace with itself. This is not because there are some heavily muscled doorkeepers that prohibit all those non-realized entities from entering. Absolutely not. The reason is very simple: The intensity of being here is so strong that the non-realized beings just stay away. Not everyone is capable of passing through a sun, you see? More-over, there is absolutely nothing one could get here. Nothing that could enrich a conditional life.

This realm is young. Well, realm is certainly not the right term – it is more a realm of realms-in-becoming. One could say Utopia is so young that its heart has barely had a few beats. Yet, there is no need to rush to come here, to be among the first who provide form to the new clay.

So what do we do out here? I'll be honest. I just love the quiet. In a sense, I am still relaxing from my incarnations. I enjoy being formless, and I continue to have great compassion for all of creation. So personally, I tend to travel more in non-Utopia, making myself available to the entities, than being out in Utopia, exploring the new ways of creation.

Right now, while we walk, feel into this peace. As a human you rarely encounter peace in such purity. On Earth, everything is constantly struggling with its life, constantly facing challenges or creating challenges out of boredom. Peace outside is not known, and peace within is seldom sought. But here – here there is peace everywhere. Within the realm itself and within the entities. From this peace, true creativity can emerge. Undistorted expression, as some call it. It provides a joy that non-realized entities can hardly relate to.

What will become of Utopia? That is up to us and up to you, once you join us. You are certainly welcome. But no matter how Utopia is going to develop, one thing is certain: Once free, always free. Whichever way consciousness chooses to unfold, free beings will remain free. You cannot un-free yourself once you have set yourself free.

You cannot forget having realized the un-realness of all of reality.

Utopia is beyond the human imagination. The fact though that you met me might help to convince you that Nirvana is not the end. Nirvana is the gateway to a new way of existence taking place in the no-place. To be with us, just let go of everything. Actually, letting go is quite simple and joyful. Joy, by the way, was one of the pillars of my teachings. The joy that comes with presence, with stillness, with letting go of all those burdens, with approaching your true self – ah, there is hardly anything more beautiful. So rejuvenating. So motivating. So fulfilling.

That sounds like some nice closing words, so we should leave it at that. Having shared this walk and talk with you was a great honor for me. With that, the Tathagata bids you farewell. Feel free to take as much peace with you as you wish. And joy also. May both be with you at all times.

Namaste.

6. Fire and Water

I am Althar, the Crystal Dragon.

I am a being who has been brought forth by Aouwa. As a dragon, it was one of my tasks to explore and guide energies. That is why I will complement his explanations in my role as an expert on energies. As we shall see, the experiences of true selves and the energy they employ cannot be separated. This also means that overcoming the standstill required a profound change at an energetic level.

The world as you experience it is based on *polarity*. Why? Because the true selves originally did not know who they were. Rather, they were in an inner struggle: *I don't want to be here! I want to go back. I don't want to exist. But if I exist, who am I? I want to find out!*

All true selves had, at the very core of their consciousness, this back and forth, this duality, this *polarity*. When a true self then went through the original alchemical transmutation and brought forth pure energy, it reflected the true self's inner state perfectly by being based on polarity. It *had* to be this way, as pure energy is just a crystallized portion of their very own consciousness.

You might be more accustomed to the term *duality*, but I prefer to use *polarity* instead, as it emphasizes the underlying energetics.

Note that I exaggerate a bit to make my point as clear as possible. It is not that pure energy would constantly be in battle with itself. Far from that! But at its core, it is based on the nature of polarity, which continues into the coarser forms of energy. Polarity is expressed quite subtly and delicately in the non-physical, and very solidly, sometimes harshly, in the physical.

So at the very beginning of consciousness in expression lies polarity, and this can be denoted as the *main characteristic of the Second Round of Creation.*

In the terminology of the dragons, we refer to the two primary principles underlying polarity as *fire* and *water*. We call them principles, because depending on the density they appear in, they have different characteristics. Yet, they can always be traced back to their very origins. More-over, *one principle cannot exist without the other.*

Fire is of an expanding nature. It appears as light, heat, or electricity, whereas water is of a contracting nature. It can become solid, it is cooling, and it is the basis for magnetism.

Everything that has ever been created in the Second Round of Creation, including the human realm, is based on the interplay of fire and water. Together, they produce all manifestations, be they seemingly static or obviously dynamic. Fire and water constantly revolve around each other and change back and forth between their extremes. Because everything consists of these two fundamentally different and conflicting principles, everything is subject to constant change.

It is as if an indestructible rubber band connects the two principles. When one principle moves away from the other, it *appears* as if it is independent of the other, but in reality it is only approaching the moment where it has to snap back to it with force. Both principles are bound to exist together. As much as they might wish, they will never be free from the other principle. The more they try, the harder they will eventually be pulled back to each other.

Humans have gained a very good understanding of polarity. They discovered so many of the rhythms, cycles, and elements all based on it. And even the Gods they created could not get along without the polarity of heavens and hells, do's and don'ts.

Humans, specifically in the East, have described polarity and its effects using terms like "Yin and Yang" or "Wheel of Life". It is widely accepted there, and very accurately so, that both principles, Yin and Yang, water and fire, carry their respective counterpart within each other. Even if a development seems to have gone completely into the direction of one principle, the other *is still there*. Not just as a potential, but as an *unescapable law* of the Second Round of Creation. Sooner or later, it will make itself palpable and strengthen. It will make sure that the dominance of the other will start to regress, by which, ultimately, everything is moving in cycles of various magnitudes.

The fact that everything is constantly changing is surely not hard to discover. Simple observation suffices to come to this obvious conclusion, and it does not even require an understanding of the cause of the change. Still, to this very day, most humans do everything they can to deny this fact. They distract themselves so that they do not have to face the reality of the omnipresent *impermanence*, and thus their own death.

Humans, and entities in general, want the pleasant things to persist, even though they know that everything is in a constant flux. They try to capture what they like and run away from what they do not like. By doing so, they deny the inevitable impermanence of everything created and resist the nature of the Second Round of Creation. They experience their resistance as *emotional friction*.

Emotional friction in the form of frustration, as well as fear of loss and impermanence, is a constant companion of every entity within the Second Round of Creation. The human though experiences emotional friction in its utmost intensity. His body is constantly exposed to potential pain. His emotions can bring him from heaven to hell in a split second. And additionally, the human has no clue of his grander reality. This is experiencing polarity at its finest.

A glance at your human news shows makes it very clear what a major part emotional friction plays in the human realm. Some eons ahead, historians will shake their heads when reviewing this strange human realm. They will ask themselves, "Was there no way to better implement the idea of embodiment?" Well, these future know-it-alls have not even had a single incarnation so far. They sit in the midst of their spiritual families, commenting on what happens on planet Earth. They wait until you and the likes of you have prepared an all-inclusive tour into embodied ascension. Ah, but if only they knew! There is nothing like being amongst the adventurers, entering new territory for the first time, right?

In a previous message, I used the term "The Wound of Creation" to denote the fact that all appearances in the Second Round of Creation are based on fire and water and thus cause emotional friction. Many true selves became aware of this wound, but for a very long time they found no way to heal it. This is another reason why they tend to deny their full creatorship. Somehow, they judge themselves, they have created a complete mess. Perhaps it would have been better not to begin with creating on a large scale. And certainly, it is better not to try again!

Some two and a half thousand years ago, philosophers thought they had found a way out of polarity and its side effects. They started to flee into the realms of *ideas*. Some proclaimed that everything that exists is the result of ideas that were thought in the mind of... well, that depended on the school of thought.

Consider a circle. What is a circle? Take a sheet of paper and draw a point somewhere on it. Now choose a distance and draw all the points having exactly the chosen distance from the original point. A human calls the result a circle, but in reality that drawing is a *reflection* or a *representation* of a circle, not a *real* circle. Why? Because you cannot even draw a point!

Whatever you draw as a point has some extension. If you zoomed in on that point, it would look like a blob of ink. No matter how small you depict a point, it will always have an extension. Hence, how could you ever draw two points having a given distance, or a whole circle consisting of an infinite number of points? All you can do is create a reflection of the idea "circle", which might be a good approximation, but never the idea itself.

In fact, you cannot even imagine a circle, because whatever you imagine also needs to have an extension. Otherwise, it would be invisible even to your inner eyes.

So in other words, a circle exists solely as an *idea*, but nowhere in creation will you find a circle! Not even in your imagination. Still, who could deny the *idea* of a circle? It has to exist in its very own non-physical realm. Moreover, the idea of a circle is *unchanging* and *perfect* in itself.

So these philosophers concluded that physical reality is just an imperfect reflection of a set of perfect ideas in the mind of "something". Humans and physicality must have fallen from the grace of the thinker of these pure ideas and should strive to get back there.

Sure enough, some schools of thought started to reject the imperfect physical world, including the body, its joys, and the beauty of experiencing physicality through it. They strived to leave all of that behind to "return home" – back into a realm of perfection and pure ideas. They had enough of bumpy circles and wanted the real thing; back to a realm where a circle would just be a circle. Damnit, if you can describe it, it has to exist, right?

But as soon as those philosophers applied their concepts not only to lifeless objects, such as circles, but also to *feelings*, it became difficult. As an example, take my favorite: beauty. They thought about it and the question came up, "Is the *idea* of beauty beautiful?"

This simple question blew away all their perfect concepts, because no matter how you answer the question, you run into contradictions. Well, I can answer it, you can certainly do it, and a pure sentimentalist would just look at these philosophers with an open mouth, eyes asking, "Really? That is your problem?" But they were stringent in their arguments, and so they found themselves stranded in a dead end. What sense would the *idea* of beauty have if the idea could not be beautiful in itself?

A circle is a static, frozen concept. Therefore, one might argue that it is solely based on the principle of water and thus *not* subject to polarity.

But this is the fallacy of the philosophers, and even more so of the mathematicians! For it is only the human mind that suffocates the circle and bans it into stagnation. The mind desperately wants to have something in existence that is invariable. It wants something stable to rely on. Such as a circle.

What an illusion!

Even though a circle appears to be static to the human mind, it is actually full of life! Create a circle for yourself right now and observe it. Feel the circle or visualize a representation of it. It doesn't matter how you do it. Then, allow your circle to change its form.

*

As you "see", *the circle changes immediately,* as soon as you allow it. The circle *loves* to change its form, because that is its very nature.

The Flower of Life is a beautiful arrangement of circles. As a pure idea though, it is dead. But breathe some fire through it and life comes to life. *However, it comes at the price of polarity.*

Don't get me wrong. I have a lot of respect for many of those original philosophers, and quite a few of them learned to go beyond their mind as soon as they became aware of the mind's innate limitations. They became real mystics. They did not deny their mind, but merely ceased to use it in areas in which it had no access.

The point I want to make here is that fleeing physical reality into the world of the mind and its perfect, ideal, yet lifeless objects is literally a dead end – back then as well as today.

The mind's idea of a circle consists of frozen water, representing one extreme of the spectrum. This holds for any mental concept, be it an idea or an ideal of whatever kind. But whatever is frozen, solidified, or stuck yearns for *life*. It yearns for *fire*, because it is still *within* the spectrum of polarity. While *appearing* to be stable, it is actually gathering momentum to return to the other pole.

Thus, the mind needs ever more energy to keep the illusion of stability!

Eventually, the apparently lifeless objects will attract the fire so massively that a mind trying to hold on to its frozen concepts will simply be swept away by a firestorm.

Nowadays, most humans do not think in terms of perfect ideas, yet they are drawn deeper and deeper into the world of the mind and its lifeless, artificial concepts. This has led to endless repetitions and refinements within the limited realm of the mind. Cycles within cycles that accelerate with any "new" technology invented by the mind itself.

But no matter what is invented by the mind, in the end, it is just fire and water performing the same old dance over and over again, ever faster and faster. Does this sound familiar? Sure it does!

It is the standstill, only in human disguise.

*

In fact, humanity is currently at a crossroads. Over the past few centuries, the human experience has been shifting more and more into the mind and is happening at an ever-increasing pace. For some this may be interesting, but for those who understand the mechanics of fire and water and who are searching for a way out of the same old patterns, it will not become any easier. They are increasingly becoming outsiders who can hardly escape the general trends. In a not-too-distant future, this may lead to Earth not being *the* place for embodied ascension.

So we have seen that everything "new" sooner or later succumbs to the cyclical bustle of fire and water. Whether with a body or without, whether with reason or without – as soon as the "new" was taken into possession, it was suddenly just as old as everything else.

Thus, simple embodiment was not enough to ward off the standstill. And how could it have been in the first place? Fire and water are just mirrors of the true selves. *Only a change of the true selves themselves could change the characteristics of fire and water!* Hence, embodied ascension remained as the last great hope of the entities to avoid the standstill.

Before turning to the energetic aspects of embodied ascension, let us once again dream our dream. For how could fire and water *ever* come into harmony without dreaming about it first?

Come! Dream with me!

Dream of fire and water in harmony.

Dream of a beauty that does not fade away.

Dream of an artist who is creating just for the sake of beauty.

Dream of unconditional love experienced and shared by entities.

What a wonderful dream. And how wonderful that it has come true.

I am Althar, a dreamer of most beautiful dreams.

7. A Simpleton

I am a simpleton.

I am not used to talk. Talking was never mine. Even back then, in my last incarnation, I did not talk. For the words of the humans never became friends of mine.

I had no teacher. Guess that was a stroke of luck. Nobody came around and wanted to explain anything to me.

Some tried. But I only looked at them. They thought me a fool. Not sure if they were right. But I felt just fine the way I was.

So I grew up as the village's simpleton. They gave me food and shelter. What more did I need?

The humans left me alone, but I was always, always, always in good company.

I sang to the stars, and they showed me history.

I sang to the Earth, and she showed me life.

I sang to the birds, and they showed me joy.

I sang to the dragons, and they showed me awe.

I had nothing, yet I was rich.

They called me a simpleton. It was my greatest blessing.

I knew when people would die. I just knew. When they left their body, I was there.

At such a moment, talk was not required. I showed them my heart. They understood.

I walked them to the stars, if they so wished. Some did. We've been friends ever since.

One night, I had a dream. The dragon came and he flew with me. He sang to me of myself. He sang to me of new worlds. He sang to me for the joy of singing. Then he looked at me with his eyes of crystal, questioningly.

Yes, I said without words. I will do that.

So I woke up from the dream. And woke up from dreaming to dream. And woke up from dreaming, dreaming, dreaming to dream.

Then I was back home.

I was a simpleton. That was my greatest blessing.

The dragon came again. Others came with him. We had a great celebration.

Are you ready, the dragon then asked without words.

And I was.

He sang to me, and we were there. There, where he brought me in that dream.

And there I've stayed ever since. Only without dreaming.

The dragon said without words, you will be the Patron of these vast fields. But I don't know what a Patron is. And I don't care. I just love to be here.

I love to create stars.

I love to create earths.

I love to create birds.

I love to love to love to love.

The dragon asked without words, have you heard of Utopia?

I don't know what that is. And I don't care.

I am still a simpleton. It serves me well.

You, who are with me right now, I have a promise for you. When your time has come. When you stop dreaming that you dream a dream. When you leave your body. Watch for me.

I will be there. You cannot miss me.

I will walk you to the stars. Or I will walk you towards the place where I am right now. Even though it is no place at all.

Whatever you choose.

Whenever you choose.

If you so choose.

You cannot miss me. I will be there.

I am a simpleton. It is my greatest blessing.

8. Fluid Light

I am Althar, the Crystal Dragon.

Let me briefly summarize my remarks on fire and water: The true selves were in an inner state of conflict, which was reflected in the pure energy being derived from them. Therefore, pure energy is based on the principles of fire and water, which mutually limit each other. In fact, *fire and water can only exist when mutually limiting each other!* They bind each other and thus force creations into repetitive cycles, patterns, and emotional friction.

Understanding this fact of life, humans came to strive for *balance*. Balance being some kind of equilibrium between two extremes, or a controlled back and forth around the zero point of a spectrum. Given the characteristics of the two principles, striving for balance is a wise choice. However, staying in balance requires a constant effort, simply because *everything* is constantly changing.

The moment a human grasps this to its fullest can be shocking! It implies that *there will be no rest for him in the known reality.* That is why a wise one once said, the awakening human has no place to lay his head.

No matter how practical balance may be in everyday life, it does not offer any escape from the eternal repetitions. The same holds for the escape into the mind, which has repeatedly proven to be a dead end.

The only resting point is the true self, the point *before* any reality. Still, apart from the fears associated with dwelling in the true self, unfulfilled desires, unresolved patterns, and the wish for happy endings or a better world all draw the human morsel of consciousness back into the world. Over and over again.

Although the true self is the only "way out", the human always finds reasons to avoid it. Even if he happens to feel it, no matter if it's while he is alive or after his physical death, after a little rest he is eager to go out again and continue the game. The resting was only temporary, providing some sense of balance at best.

Fortunately, among the many incarnating beings, there were also those who had achieved non-embodied ascension in the non-physical areas. They had recognized the Principle of Ascension and wanted to repeat it on Earth. However, these beings, like all others who incarnated as human beings, also suffered a complete amnesia. They had completely forgotten who they were, where they came from, and what they wanted on Earth.

But throughout the course of many incarnations, some succeeded in feeling the longing for their own true self even while being embodied. They vaguely recalled that instead of getting caught in external distractions, they could also go within. Some began to open up, and so gradually they went deeper and deeper into themselves. They approached their own emptiness and faced the fear that is so often caused by it.

And at some point, it happened: *The first human realized his true self!* He liberated himself from the bonds of fire and water and found peace within. All questions disappeared. All doubt disappeared. Even the breath of doubt, which had remained after the non-embodied ascension, dissolved. And through the enlightenment of that human, *his true self changed fundamentally.*

His fundamentally new state as an ascended being *had* to be reflected by his pure energy. And so a new alchemical transmutation took place:

Fire and water blended and created something totally new: fluid light.

*

So on an energetic level, embodied ascension resulted in the blending of fire and water into fluid light, which exhibits fundamentally *new* characteristics. Because of these new characteristics, some use the term "new energy", but to me, fluid light sounds more beautiful and appropriate. In addition, it triggers so many soothing sensations.

As much as I would like to give you a taste of fluid light, I simply cannot. But perhaps you can sense the fundamentally new potentials that have become available with the emergence of fluid light.

Creation, as you know it, is based on the limitations of polarity, implying impermanence and emotional friction in all of its facets. Fluid light, however, is completely different.

Fluid light is unlimited!

It is not bound by an opposing force!

It is beyond polarity, cycles, and patterns!

It does not cause any emotional friction!

In other words:

Fluid light enables undistorted creation!

Thus, the standstill is overcome.

*

Fluid light has come into a constant *harmony within itself*, as is the true self that has brought it forth.

Try to feel the difference! To do so, consider an old energy particle. It is in balance, but that balance is like a prison. It is a truce of the two principles that are bound to each other for an indefinite period of time.

In contrast, fluid light is in *harmony*. There is no struggle within it. Although it emerged from the principles of fire and water, it is so much more.

Metaphorically speaking, fluid light can expand in any direction *without any limitation!* It can always move on and on and develop. No rubber band will snap it back. No embedded impermanence will cause creations of fluid light to be subject to decay. What incredible new possibilities for expression!

Utopia, the no-place, is the realm of realms where fluid light is used for creation. It is the no-place where ascended beings experience unlimited, undistorted creation.

Utopia is ascended consciousness in expression.

Can you feel the excitement? Can you feel the *new* potentials? Can you feel why the standstill has been overcome? Can you feel why speaking of the Third Round of Creation is so appropriate?

For a long time, this was only a dream.

Before we started dreaming, we looked at that very first particle of physical matter. Maybe, so it was thought, if energy could become more dense, then maybe it could become even lighter. Maybe fire and water could come into harmony.

We held on to that dream. And then, suddenly, it realized itself. Suddenly, the standstill was no more. Yes, individual true selves might experience it. For a while. *But creation as such moved on.* Embodied ascension and the resulting emergence of fluid light have made this possible.

What a dream.

Time to wake up. Come! See for yourself!

*

Now, of course, the question arises whether fluid light can also be used in the human realm.

As far as we know, it cannot – at least not directly. But apart from the purely practical difficulties, one must not forget that the human realm has been designed, structured, and co-created by a multitude of beings for a very specific purpose. This order should not be easily disturbed. And why would you want to, anyway? To pay your rent? You are kidding, right? Generally speaking, fluid light and human mass consciousness are currently so fundamentally different that it cannot be used on Earth.

However, being aware of Utopia and of the existence of fluid light can affect your life even before you realize ascension. Why? Because it releases you from so many burdens! The standstill is no more, so there is no need to rescue existence, the world, or even yourself. The dream has already become true, so you can relax and step out of your own way. This alone will allow for a drastic change in the way you experience daily life. Just be *present! Cultivate being present!* Be aware of your true self while acting on the human stage.

Then, suddenly, even the notion of friction loses its annoying characteristics. Suddenly, you are not just moving in and out of your true self, but you are in constant awareness of it. Suddenly, you end the dream. Suddenly, you are in Utopia. Suddenly, you are a New Magi. Suddenly, you walk the Earth as an embodied ascended human being and recognize:

Experiencing Utopia and fluid light while at the same time having a human body on Earth is possible!

If this is realized by many humans, it may change the human realm in the long term in such a way that fluid light can also be applied there. But this should not be your concern. While you are walking the Earth, simply be *all* that you are. Your presence will make you an Ambassador of Utopia without you having to speak a single word. This non-language is understood by those who are ready for it. This non-language is understood by fire and water, and both will be at your service.

There is nothing you can *do* to make this happen. Realize that cultivating your presence is not a *doing*. It is just being in awareness of all that is, of all that *you* are, which will ultimately and naturally bring forth embodied ascension and fluid light.

I am Althar, a dragon of fluid light.

9. Love of Self

I am Echnatara.

You might remember me from the story told by Althar when he spoke about releasing the Atlantean trauma. He has invited me to share with you what happened in my last lifetime in Atlantis, and as far as possible, afterwards. I have not been incarnated since then, and have to admit that expressing in the human language is no longer easy for me. But the dragon – as we simply called him at the time – has assured me that you, dear reader, will be very capable of relating to my words on a level that goes far beyond their purely literal meaning. So with this I happily accept the invitation and hope that my story will be interesting and inspiring for you.

I grew up in the same community as Althar. Much like him, I soon began to develop a feeling of being different from the other members of the community, of not really belonging to them. Presumably, many humans feel this at a young age, because being incarnated is actually something very unnatural. However, most seem to simply ignore this feeling. They settle into the environment they find themselves in and focus on the necessities and joys of human life, rather than hanging on to that peculiar feeling of strangeness.

Our community was focused on exploring the ways of energies. This fundamental attitude served us very well. We gained deep insights into the rhythms of nature and skillfully learned to use them to produce food in abundance. We also invented many helpful technologies that simplified our daily lives.

My personal nature, however, was not that of a researcher. Rather, I tended to approach life in an intuitive way. I simply couldn't relate to this urgent desire of the others wanting to *understand* everything. Although I saw the results that came from dissecting and analyzing nature, and even profited from them, it felt for me somehow "just not right". It seemed that an essential part was missing in all these research projects, but I couldn't say what it was.

That is the problem with being intuitive: Often times you cannot convey what you *just know*, and you cannot even grasp it yourself. Especially if you are still young and have not yet learned to deal with it, being intuitive is not always easy and sometimes even leads to complications with your fellow human beings.

At that time, there was a fairly young "Master of the Energies" in our community, who was about ten years older than me. He had reincarnated, bringing with him many of the insights and talents he already had in his previous lifetimes. A special gift of his was his clarity, which enabled him to grasp even the most complex circumstances. Being in a very supportive environment, he was able to allow his gifts to unfold very fast, and in fact became the youngest Master of the Energies the community ever had. As you might have guessed, his name was Althar.

At first sight, Althar seemed to be the proto-type of the ideal researcher. It appeared as if he was made to serve the primary interest of the community and to work on a better understanding of the energies. A wonderful future seemed to await him.

However, despite these apparently ideal circumstances, there was often an aura of unease around him. His very talents were probably the reason why he started quite early to question the ways of the community. The sole exploration of the *expression* of the energies was secondary to him. Rather, he had a strong intuition and conviction that there had to be a *source of energy*. An origin of all energy, even before it divided into different kinds of energies. Finding that source of energy was what really interested him and what he wanted to pursue. But he simply did not succeed in evoking the same passion or even interest in the others that he had for this question.

I attended various meetings in which Althar spoke to the community about his intuition and his wish to devote himself entirely to this quest. But he had nothing to substantiate it! He had nothing to show us. He could not even promise any advantage to the community should he find that source. And why would one need a source of energy anyway when energy was abundantly available *everywhere?*

You have to understand that while we had no limiting religious beliefs, the commonly accepted notion of the world was that everything was energy, and that energy constantly changed from one form to another. This seemed to be an obvious fact which could be confirmed by everyone who had eyes. And this transformation of energy even took place across whole sequences of lifetimes, as the young, embodied Master of the Energies proved by his own existence.

So Althar became increasingly frustrated and started to become more and more of an annoyance for the whole community. At that time, I could very much relate to his state of being. His idea of a source of energy did not exactly attract me, but I shared his intuition that there had to be something beyond the interplay of energies. Why else would I feel so foreign *being* in these energies?

One day, Althar declared to the community that he wanted to be on his own in the mountains for a longer period of time. He wanted to be totally isolated, not to be affected by anyone's ideas, beliefs, or by the necessity to comply with modes of conduct that had been established in the community. Only then, so was his argument and hope, could he reach beyond the energies.

The community liked that idea. They agreed immediately as it was good for everyone. Althar would be off, no longer disturbing community life. If he succeeded, well, perhaps it would be of interest for all of them. If he failed, he could return and reassume his role as Master of the Energies. The hope was that in any case, he would have freed himself from his obsession.

It was agreed that every ten days someone would hike up to his mountain hut to bring food, avoiding any interaction with him. When the question was asked, who would be willing to take care of the supply, my arm lifted as if on its own. I had not even thought about it. It was just right.

That moment marked the beginning of our common journey, though at the time, neither him nor I had any idea how far it would lead us. Althar was just happy to immerse himself into pursuing his dream of finding the source of energy, and I was happy to support someone I felt a certain bond with. That same day, Althar set out into the mountains. There was simply nothing that could have kept him in the village any longer.

My own life began to change completely as well. Or rather, my *inner* life changed. Even though it took a long time until Althar and I spoke to each other, I was in a certain way continually with him. I constantly felt him in his hut, and sensed the ups and downs of his moods. Even though it was a half-day hike to the hut, the spatial distance did not affect my ability to perceive him.

It was particularly striking that as soon as I went up to his place in the mountains every ten days, I felt a certain clarity rising within me. It was not that I suddenly found joy in science or research; I still had no wish to quantify or develop and test models. But being in connection with him also created a connection with his clarity. This made it much easier for me to discern the various intuitions of my inner being. Until then, they had often intermingled with each other, which made me feel confused or even frustrated. I did not know *how* my clarity became enhanced, I did not care *why* it happened, but I enjoyed the effects very much.

Later, we understood this phenomenon better and called it the *principle of radiance*. In a certain way, a person in awareness of himself changes not only the space around him, but also that of the people connected with him from afar. This causes their clouds of emotions and thoughts to dissolve like mist in the morning sun. Presence is contagious and naturally produces clarity.

As I said, it seemed to me that I was constantly participating in his efforts and moods. That's why I somehow felt I was an important support for him, even if I only went to him every ten days. But he did not seem to notice any of this and apparently had not even registered me as a person. The agreement stated that I should put down the supplies fifty steps in front of the hut as to not disturb him. In spite of this, as soon as he spotted me from a distance, he either retreated into his hut or went up the mountain.

Nevertheless, I have always enjoyed the hike to him. I was closer to him than the other nine days, and I could feel the impact of his presence even more clearly. Besides, I had the opportunity to leave the community and everyday life behind me, and thus could reconsider my role in life from a distance.

After about a dozen ten-day cycles, I noted a heaviness developing around the hut, which became more and more pronounced over the next few weeks. So much so that I started worrying about Althar's state of mind. So far, we had not had any contact at all. We had not spoken to each other, there was no exchange of eye contact, and not even a greeting from afar. Although I understood and respected his underlying idea, this dark emotional cloud looming around the hut made me increasingly uncomfortable. What could I do?

One day, courageously, instead of simply unpacking my backpack in the usual place and immediately turning back, I sat down and pretended to be exhausted. Sitting there, I expanded my own energy field and embraced the dark cloud, including the hut. I was very surprised when I felt a movement that suddenly came into the gloom! It was like airing a stuffy room, so I knew I was doing the right thing. I sat there for a while and was grateful to be able to return some of what I had received in the last few months through his presence.

Somehow that event became a turning point, not just for me, but also for him. Later, Althar told me, at that time he had arrived at a point of total exhaustion. He had searched everywhere for the source of energy without even finding the slightest trace of it. In his disappointment, he had begun to mock himself, for what should a title like "Master of the Energies" signify if he did not even know where the energies came from? His search had led him into isolation and affliction. A mental breakdown followed by madness would come next. Continuing his search in this form made no sense. And as bitter as it was for him, he finally decided, after a long struggle, to surrender. He let go of his idea of a source of energy.

At that moment, so he told me later his version of the incident, when he made this decision, he began to relax – for the first time in so many years! At the same time, he could feel the whole atmosphere around him brighten up. And suddenly, as though out of nowhere, an insight arose in him. It became clear that he had searched for the source of energy everywhere *outside* of himself, but never *within!* This was the only remaining place he had not yet explored. This realization gave him new hope and his passion was back instantly. He would continue his search in this entirely new direction. And who knew what else there was within him to discover? When he realized this turning point, he looked out of the hut's window and saw how I was just getting up from my "break" and making my way back.

Maybe it was just a coincidence, maybe that idea would have come to him anyway, or maybe my supportive, accepting energy had helped him. Ultimately, it doesn't matter. But from that point on, he changed. I didn't notice him observing me when I left, but for some reason, I carried a bright smile on my face while returning to the village.

During my next two visits to the hut, I did not see him at all, but the atmosphere around the hut had become much lighter. Then, when I came in sight of the hut on the following visit, I saw him sitting outside, leaning against a large boulder. He appeared to be at peace with himself. This time he did not run away, but smiled at me and gestured for me to come to him. With each step closer, it became more obvious that something extraordinary had happened to him. Unsure what to do, I just sat next to him and we enjoyed the great view of the valley. After a while he asked, "What is your name?"

"My name is Echnatara," I answered.

"Echnatara – *she who sends out existence*. A beautiful name."

"Yes. I like it very much."

We sat in silence for a while.

"Echnatara," he said, looking at me with his dark eyes.

"Yes?"

"Thank you. Thank you for all you did."

I nodded with a smile.

Even though I was very curious, I did not ask him what had changed him so much. I did not want to disturb the precious silence we were sharing. So we sat together for a while and simply gazed into the valley. When it was time for my return, we looked into each other's eyes and I left. This was our first real encounter. Only a few words were spoken, yet so much had happened.

While I went home, I made a deep choice. Whatever it was that Althar had experienced, I wanted to experience the same! The transformation he had undergone was so deep and felt so *right*, I just knew it would also be right for my life. I trusted my intuition.

The next ten days felt like an eternity. I longed to see him again. Maybe next time Althar would be willing to share something about his journey? In any case, I wanted to convey my sincere interest in his experiences.

When the ten days had finally passed and I arrived at his hut, I was shocked to see the door open and Althar lying on the floor. I ran to him, fearing he might have died. When I reached his body, I was happy to find that he was breathing, although he was unconscious. Despite the difficult situation, I was certain that everything would be all right. I knew I need not touch him or sprinkle his face with water or anything like that. So I sat next to him and waited. And waited. And waited.

After a few hours, when dusk had already fallen, he woke up and looked around in confusion. He did not know where he was. When he saw me, he seemed to remember. His eyes told me, *Echnatara, please, take me in your arms.* And so I did.

A few months later, after I went through a similar transformational experience, he told me what he had experienced while he lay unconscious on the floor. At that time he was in the midst of his true self, accompanied by his dear friend, the dragon. Althar became aware of the vastness of the omniverse, the boundless potentials, and the ways of creation. He became aware of a dream that his true self dreamed together with so many other entities: the dream of embodied ascension. And the dragon urged him to make a choice: A choice either to give up his human body or to return to it and live the dream of his true self in physical reality. He could not delay this decision for long, for the longer he remained outside of his body, the more difficult it would become to return to it.

Dear reader, because I went through a very similar experience as Althar, I must admit that it is impossible to convey the difficulty this choice represents to a being. The greatness and beauty in the true self and in other realities are simply too overwhelming. The temptation to be once again without the limits, needs, and pains of a body and to be back home again is so great that a human being cannot imagine it. If you have experienced the limited human existence, then found your way back and realized your own oneness, why should you reassume a human form?

I can only guess that it was even more difficult for Althar than it was for me, because his true self was one of those who held the dream of embodied ascension. That is why he felt bound by a promise that the true selves had given each other at that time. A promise to help other humans in their ascension. But while he remembered this promise, he doubted at the same time that help was at all possible. For how could you convey something as overwhelming as "You are creation"?

Then, the dragon invited him to look at the indescribable panorama of potentials. They were all around him like stars in the night sky. The dragon prompted him to focus his attention on a tiny, tiny point in this panorama and to dive deeper and deeper into this potential. When he did, he started to recognize within it the mountains of our homeland, then his hut, then his human body, as he lay on the floor of the hut. Finally, he saw me sitting beside him, worried. That was the moment he made the choice to come back. "At least I should try," he thought. And so he did.

It took him a while to readjust to the human reality. One might think that for a being having opened up his consciousness so much, living in physical reality would be a smooth ride. Not at all! Far from it, because not only the humans and their ways of being are often times hard to bare, but also one's own body holds so many deeply rooted conditionings and patterns that do not suddenly vanish, even if they are not needed anymore. The body is a biological vessel that is designed for long-term survival. It does not change instantly, only because its occupant has adopted a broader perspective. Rather, the adaptation takes time and is often unpleasant. By the way, this is a major reason why a spiritual development is frequently so difficult and accompanied by so many ups and downs.

Althar recognized this circumstance intuitively and remained in the hut for quite a while so he could become familiar with his new way of being, and to give his body the necessary time to adapt prior to returning to the community. But during this time, he began to actively accompany me on my way.

For me, it was a blessing to have witnessed Althar's development, because it made my own so much smoother. Even in difficult moments, I always knew through him that I was not simply following a fantasy. He made it easy for me by never explaining anything. He knew that using words would only generate expectations, and that expectations have the tendency to realize themselves. He also knew that my character was very different from his. I did not have his scientific nature and was not exactly interested in abstract explanations of my own experiences.

So instead of talking, we simply sat together and held eye contact. This was the most natural way through which we could share our presence. When he went into his presence, the energies around him changed and a kind of bubble manifested, embracing both of us. Being in the bubble was like being in a very different reality. Then it was very easy for me to harmonize with him and to develop a very similar presence. As a result, a kind of upward spiraling developed, in which we could both open up more and more. And that was just beautiful.

Althar told me that the dragon had often done this type of exercise with him. Because when you are ready to let go and open up, it is of immense help when a loving being is near. So Althar assumed for me the role the dragon had played for him.

One day, while we were doing this exercise together in the hut, I sensed the dragon myself for the first time. *Old,* I thought, *so old. This dragon can wait. Year after year. Thousands of years. Immobile. He waits. He observes. He accepts. He accepts everything. And then, when the time has come, he takes off. He spreads his wings and flies. And now he is here.*

Suddenly, the dragon took us with him and the three of us flew together. We left the world and even physical reality behind us. Then, suddenly, the dragon moved around his own axis and we dove into an ocean of colors. Colors that do not exist on Earth. Colors from flowing, radiant light. They arranged themselves in ever new patterns and formations. They gained depth and created vistas. They responded to every movement of the dragon. It was breathtakingly beautiful in a very literal sense.

When we were finally back in physical reality, I was stunned and could hardly catch my breath. It took me a while to collect myself. Then I asked Althar, "Tell me, can one die of beauty?"

He glanced to the ceiling of the hut, then looked at me. "Yes," he said. "Easily. You need a really good reason to return here from such beauty."

I nodded. "So it is very good that I have a reason." I took his hands into mine. "Promise me, Althar... do not leave without me."

"Yes, I promise." he said. Then he looked within and added more to himself, "I already promised that a very long time ago."

When Althar was ready to return to the community, we moved together into a small temple which we called the "Temple of Beauty". The others realized that Althar had changed very much, but most of them attributed this to the fact that he had apparently fallen in love with me. They were joking amongst each other, for they knew this specific "Source of Energy" themselves. But it was not malicious joking. Everyone was glad Althar was back and that he was doing well.

Althar himself supported this assessment by the others, because it meant he did not have to explain to anyone what had actually happened to him. He simply went on exploring the ways of energies, but now from his grander perspective. Only slowly did he start to inspire visitors of the temple to go within. The concept of exploring one's own consciousness was so alien to most visitors that he needed to discern very carefully who would be ready for it. Over a period of time, however, there were some who felt that Althar was different in an intriguing way. They became curious and opened up more and more to him and his subtle instructions.

Althar and I also continued our common exercises and journeys into other realms of life, and so we grew accustomed to these greatly expanded states of consciousness. For me, these journeys were the ideal preparation for what was to come. In a sense, they "stretched" all my assumptions about reality, or simply dissolved them.

One day, when I was sitting alone in the temple in pure awareness, it suddenly felt like I was falling into me. While I fell and fell, everything external faded away. But then I realized that I was not falling *at all*. There was nothing that *could* fall, because I had no body! I had no center! And yet I was aware of my beingness. I was my beingness before any outer appearances.

And then the most beautiful thing happened: *An overwhelming love arose in my beingness.* A love from me for me. There was nothing I could have directed that love to, nothing that sent love to me. This love was simply there. My love. That was me. I existed before anything, yet in love with myself. What an incomparable experience!

As I surrendered to my own love for myself, I suddenly became aware of all that I ever was and of all that I ever could be. All of that was my *real* I, my true self. It was my true self in expression, experiencing itself. I clearly saw the polarity in the creations and the limitations caused by them. And I saw another way of existing and expressing, beyond polarity, beyond opposites.

This is where I wanted to go! But then I remembered Althar and what he had done for me. I remembered the mission he had taken on. So I postponed my desire to go into this new kind of existence and made the choice to return to him. The awareness of my love for myself, however, stayed with me even on Earth and has not left me ever since.

When Althar saw me later that day, he knew immediately what had happened to me, and we fell into each other's arms.

I have to admit, I only came back because Althar was so close to me. I felt no obligation to help other people on their way, because ultimately I have a deep confidence in the natural unfolding of each individual's existence. But I could very well understand Althar's argument when he said it would be extremely difficult for a human, let alone for all other beings, to let go of all the distractions and turn within. Without inspiration and without other beings that had shown ascension could be accomplished, a human would probably have little chance. And even he himself had only succeeded due to very favorable circumstances.

Maybe he was right. I, however, was only certain that the presence of an enlightened person could be very helpful, for I had experienced it myself. That's why I supported him as best I could in his work in the temple.

In the following years Althar succeeded in anchoring intents within crystals. Even though the reasons why he did that were absolutely noble, this started a development which finally culminated in threats and violence by neighboring communities. One day, when Althar was in the mountains, a large group of attackers came into our village. When I saw them coming, I knew instantly what would happen. So I left the physical reality even before they destroyed our Temple of Beauty and killed my human body, as well as all the other members of the community.

As much as I wanted Althar to come with me, I quickly realized that he would not. He felt from a distance what was happening to me and the whole community, and went into a state of shock that blocked all of my attempts to communicate with him. The events befell him so vehemently and the feelings of shame and guilt were so strong that he began to immediately withdraw into a bubble of his consciousness.

What could I do? I remembered the dark cloud that had surrounded his hut. But now it was not emotions that enveloped him, but a veil of his own consciousness. So I came up with the idea of projecting my love into his gloomy "bubble of shame". I felt how my projected love turned into a kind of crystal in his bubble. A crystal as if made from fluid light. I just knew, sooner or later, he would perceive my love and know I was still connected with him. Sooner or later, he would understand that ultimately no one can take responsibility for the decisions of others. Sooner or later, he would simply move on, perhaps with a little support from his true self, or the dragon, or a future self, or a parallel stream of events.

And indeed, it actually happened. Not so long ago, Althar freed himself with a little support. Who knows? Maybe one day he will tell his whole story in his own words.

After I had left my body, I moved on to experience the realm beyond polarities. Well, what can I say about it, knowing that Utopia, as the dragon calls it, is so very different for every entity coming here. Here there are no rhythms, cycles, or repetitions as they prevail in all of the other realms, and to which every entity is subject to as soon as it gets there. In Utopia, everything *remains* new and fresh, if that makes any sense to you. Here there is just no decay. And when the human mind assumes that this results in a huge pile of stuck energies and creations, it is completely wrong. In Utopia, there is a constant, joyous expansion of every creation. *All* keeps moving! *We* keep moving.

My intuition tells me to leave it with that and to simply invite you to relate to Althar's and my story. Creation relies very much on the fact that entities can relate to experiences already made by others. There is no need to go through all experiences on your own, specifically not the difficult ones. If some entity already had an experience, one can empathize with it to a degree and move on from there.

So maybe you can empathize with the love I have found within myself for myself. Maybe you can empathize with the journey Althar and I shared. And maybe you can somehow sense me now, existing beyond polarity, enjoying totally new ways of creation. Undistorted creation, as the dragon calls it, sounds a bit sterile. Yet try to feel what it would mean *to you* if there was but a single reason for everything you create or experience: *Because you enjoy it!* Not to survive. Not because you need it to balance any kind of lack. Not to distract you. But purely because you enjoy it.

Could there be anything more beautiful?

Oh, and let me mention that the love of self continues to unfold. As a human being, I once felt that I could die of too great beauty. As an ascended being, I have realized that the ever-evolving beauty of love of self is the source of life for consciousness and creation itself.

Althar, and those who came before and after him, provided a tremendous service to existence by paving the way beyond polarity into a new way of existing. They realized the dream of their true selves of embodied ascension, and inspired others to do the same.

If you, dear reader, are also one of those holding this dream, then maybe it is time for you to wake up from it and to go within. When you come to make the choice of choices, please consider, despite all the challenges, staying embodied for a while. Not to save anyone, but simply to inspire others through your presence to unfold their own presence. Just as Althar inspired me. Just as both of us have inspired others in the Temple of Beauty.

For even if a being has experienced presence or love of self only once, and be it in another human, then the seed is planted, and sooner or later it will grow and blossom.

That is the natural way.

I am Echnatara, she who sends out existence.

10. The Illusion of a Better World

I am Althar, the Crystal Dragon.

A human approaching enlightenment often feels the state of the world as very challenging. He wishes to help make the world a better place. He is certain that so much of the sorrow done by humans to each other and the environment is not necessary.

But what is "better" though? Is my "better" better than your "better"? If so, what would you suggest I do to overcome your notion of "better"? What would you allow someone else to do so that the best "better" manifests?

Planet Earth is currently inhabited by billions of humans, each of them being at a different level of experience and wisdom. And the number of humans is constantly increasing. Earth is so attractive because it is a unique place to gather wisdom. That is why so many entities come here to incarnate.

So what would be the point in telling those who have just entered the adventure playground that they are delusional? That their concepts of reality are based on false assumptions and that there are much "better" ones? By what right should they be refused the opportunity to create experiences according to their beliefs, knowing that what they choose corresponds to their level of wisdom?

If you have children, you know firsthand that parents cannot transfer their wisdom to their children. Parents may imprint some openness, some behavioral structures, even curiosity, but then the children need to go beyond their upbringing and have their very own experiences.

Also, the conveying of wisdom within groups is very difficult. Even if a group is seeking enlightenment together, it is prone to the usual group dynamics. How could it be otherwise if they are not yet enlightened? Each tries to compensate for whatever he feels he is lacking. The paradox is that the more attractive the leader of the group, the larger the group will become and therefore, the stronger the group dynamics will play out.

Without the experience of deathlessness and without the certainty of the dreamlike nature of any reality, *any "better" society is founded on false assumptions.* Therefore, it must necessarily disintegrate sooner or later. It was just another common experience in the polarity of fire and water.

In order to avoid that the desire for a better world becomes a source of grief for him, he must deeply realize that ultimately, the idea of a "better" world is an illusion. The world is merely a reflection of what people currently want to experience. Not everyone has to experience all experienceable themselves, but nevertheless many beings choose extreme and difficult life paths for a variety of reasons. But no matter what they choose, sooner or later they will transmute it into wisdom. In this sense, the world is absolutely perfect exactly as it is.

In other words, *there is no need for a better world!*

In the face of all these circumstances, our almost- enlightened person is in an awkward position. How can he survive in such a world? Wisdom is not transferable and "better" is an illusion. But the more he succeeds in simultaneously being in the human body and in the limitlessness of his true self, the more his human incarnation feels as if it were out of place on Earth.

If you, dear reader, arrive at this point, I recommend that you repeatedly isolate yourself for a time, as to escape from the harsh mass consciousness. When you finally realize your true self, you will gain a more holistic perspective of the nature of the world and the journey of the true selves in human bodies. This naturally provides true compassion for your fellow beings and greater acceptance.

But then you will also face the choice whether you want to stay in your human body, in the midst of humans who are caught in their games. At the same time, Utopia is open to you. A whole new world of experiences is waiting for you to explore it. Although it is not an either-or decision, meaning you can experience both Utopia and the human world simultaneously, Utopia is so tempting that in the past many have given up their human body.

In some traditions, people have made a vow to remain among the humans even after their enlightenment. Although the intention behind it is certainly noble, such a vow is ultimately a contradiction in itself. Self-liberation and vows do not really go well together.

Many of those who have dreamed the dream of embodied ascension as a way to realize their true self and to birth a new creativity try to stay. Against all odds! Even though it might be harsh, why rush out? Now that the true self is realized after spending so many lifetimes in limitation, why not continue a while in non-limitation?

But defiance alone will not sustain the decision for any long period of time. Instead, it is more helpful to *nurture the wish* to return to the humans *before that moment of choice presents itself.* How about the wish to experience the light body in physical reality? Or to fulfill some of your long-cherished human desires, but without the hustle of false identities pulling the strings in the background? Any wish that is only about you is a good wish.

Even though as a dragon I will never have to make this choice, in the next chapter I would like to tell you about my greatest joy. A joy that I can only experience while being close to humans, and thus it nurtures my wish to remain near them.

I am Althar, without any doubt the best Crystal Dragon.

11. My Greatest Joy

I am Althar, the Crystal Dragon.

I would like to describe a joy which can be experienced most impressively on Earth. I have been around the cosmos quite a bit, and can therefore say that no other place is known to me in which this joy can be experienced in such purity.

As I have already admitted, I am a lover of beauty. Although each experience of beauty is unique and wonderful in itself, there is one kind of beauty I love the most:

Observing the beauty of a consciousness opening up.

To me, there is nothing like it! The shine in the eyes and energy field of a human who suddenly comes to an inner opening is outstandingly beautiful to me. This is one of the reasons why I love being around humans so much, no matter what they are acting out at any given moment.

Each inner opening, each letting go has this effect. It does not require the big, ultimate enlightenment. *Every* opening of consciousness, *every* letting go of limitations creates such a moment of exceptional beauty. Having the opportunity to witness this is my greatest joy.

I want to make a promise: Once you realize embodied ascension, you become a catalyst for others. Neither do you have to speak a single word, nor do you have to try to improve the world. In a sense, your presence alone will make the world a better place, for you will be a living potential for others, radiating unlimited existence. Even though the still-limited humans cannot really grasp *what* you radiate, your presence will point to a completely different way of being. You will become like a window through which others can look towards Utopia.

To this very day, the road to ascension passes through the human world. That might change in the future, but some of those who are incarnated right now have a chance to realize ascension in their current lifetime. For these humans, you – someone who has done it, a New Magi walking on Earth – might be the greatest inspiration they could ever encounter.

Simply radiate what you are, and maybe you can then share my greatest joy: Enjoying the beauty that arises when consciousness opens up.

As a dragon, I will remain close to the human realm, no matter what. Yes, I go here and there and everywherc, but the humans, well, I just love these crazy creatures. So expect me to be nearby in the future as well.

A final thought. There are favorable circum-stances allowing an opening of consciousness to be easier. This includes, in particular, when like-minded humans come together to share stillness. As soon as they let go of the distractions and simply join in presence, an upward spiraling is created. The presence of the others enhances their own presence. There is a deep, transforming magic in the still gaze of humans which makes it much easier to let go, to enter into one's own emptiness, and also to choose to remain embodied.

Between you and me, you should see the beauty of such a gathering from the non-physical side. *Incredible! Unparalleled!* So why not enjoy this most exquisite beauty of existence while being in the midst of it? Just a thought.

*

My dear friend, we have traveled a long way together throughout these messages. It is my great wish to thank you that I could be by your side during this journey. So much has happened beyond the words, and time and time again, I have been able to observe amazing beauty. To be honest, I did not expect that we could get so far and that I would encounter so much beauty.

Right now you might notice that we are not alone. Many friends are here to celebrate with you. So many ascended beings and so many dragons are around us. Even the Patron of Utopia is here, still not knowing what that is. Well, it is a title of honor for the first being who has realized embodied ascension. It just ended its dream and made the Third Round of Creation a reality. And so may you.

I am Althar, so happy to share with you my greatest joy.

12. Creation in Movement

I am a true self.
I have always been.
I will continue to be.

I am the ultimate observer,
I am the ultimate experiencer.
Yet, I never moved.
Indeed, I never moved.
For the point before creation
has no body.

To experience,
I send forth emanations.
Be they rays, dragons, humans, or ideas.
They dive into realities.
Some self-created, others co-created.

Are those emanations me?
They are not different from me.
Yet they are sovereign.
Sovereign, in every respect.

At some point each emanation
longs to come back to me.
To be whole again.

Like a wave,
assuming a wave-identity for a while.
Experiencing being a wave.
The movement, the dynamics, the encounters.

Then, to come back to me,
nothing special is required.
Just a change of perspective.

A perspective that is always available:
The wave sees itself
as not being different from the ocean.

Never was.
Yet, its existence was so *real*.
The experience so *rich*.

And all the time,
I was observing.
I was co-experiencing.

Observing the ways of existence.
Exploring the known and the unknown.
On my own and together with others.
And all the time,
I was coming to know myself.

Whatever can be experienced,
whatever is livable,
sooner or later it will be experienced
by a bold being.
That is the nature of creation.

And so we dived into experiences.
And so *you* dived into experiences.
Until we noted the repetitions.
Until wisdom had built its own momentum.

Now I ask you, dear human:
Can you just change your perspective?

For the time has come
to explore a new round of creation.
Creation has matured and moves on.

It moves to no-place.
You want to join?
Then simply allow your dream to be real.

Can you fathom that simplicity?
Can you allow that truth of truths?
Can you embody that truth?
Can you walk that truth in your reality?
Can you embody your true self?

For then it could be said,
you birthed yourself.
By doing so,
you birthed your true self.
By doing so,
your true self gained a body.

A body of all of its emanations, experiences,
and new potentials.
A body awakened to its very true self.
A body of consciousness.
A human body,
embodying ascended consciousness.

Then your true self could say
for the very first time:
I move.

And indeed it could be said:
Creation is in movement.

Dear human,
you want to join the no-place?
It is just a choice away.
The boldest choice a human can ever make.

I am a true self,
on the brink of being birthed by a human.

Thank you, human.
Thank you for all you did.

*

Acknowledgment

I would like to express once again my heartfelt gratitude to Tess "Serene" Henry for her continual encouragement during the creation process and support in editing the manuscript.

Thanks, Serene!

51371019R00063

Made in the USA
Lexington, KY
03 September 2019